# THE BLOOD OF KINGS

An Anthology

# THE BLOOD OF KINGS

## An Anthology

JB BROWN

**FireStep**
Press

FireStep Press an imprint of
FireStep Publishing

Gemini House
136-140 Old Shoreham Road
Brighton
BN3 7BD

www.firesteppublishing.com

First published in Great Britain by
FireStep Publishing, 2012
ISBN 978-1-908487-21-6
© JB Brown, 2012
A catalogue record for this book is available from the British Library.

Typeset by Graham Hales, Derby
Cover by Ryan Gearing

Printed and Bound in Great Britain CPI Group (UK) Ltd, Croydon, CR0 4YY

# Dedication

To those who serve and those who have served with honour.
There are none better.

# Contents

*Instead, I sometimes recall a passage from the Book of Psalms. I have no theological insight, my religious ethos is a battered one; but those lines seem to suggest an answer my reason cannot, namely that the innocent that suffer for the rest of us become anointed and loved by God in special way; the votive candle of their lives has made them heaven's prisoners.*

**James Lee Burke, Heaven's Prisoners**

*All are lunatics, but he who can analyze his delusion is called a philosopher.*

**Ambrose Bierce**

## Acknowledgements

My grandfather who started it all.
My wife, Angálica. who kept me on the straight and narrow.
My friends who encouraged me.
A gifted teacher when I was fifteen.
The women who loved me and those who broke my heart.
Ryan Gearing, who had the faith to see this through.
Soldiers, dead and alive; my friends, my calling.

# Prologue

## The Blood of Kings

Remember the halcyon days?
There was drinking of
The blood of kings.

That was before the ecdysiast
Plagued horizons,
With foreign call.
Giving nothing.
Saying nothing. Promising
Nothing.

There were, however, no muniments
To testify to this sacramental partaking.
It was and always will be
A fragmented draft,
This Blood of Kings.

# i. Beginning the Reign

## Lost In Bohemia

Train station.
Lovers saying
Sad au revoir.
In a city
Of a million different
Souls wandering.

Where are you
When I am here,
Lost and blind?
There are fragments
Of you and I
Lost in Bohemia.

And I am truly alone
In Prague.
Surely
The city for lovers
To meander together
Through clumsy architecture.

## Opposites Attract

There is no return
From riding the cohort whirlwind.

I hope when I met you,
I enriched your life.
I hope when you left me,
A glimmer of you died.

I look,
At a lake of murder.
I wade,
Into the fear.

## A Small Untruth

Remember once I stared at you?
Love searing in my eye.
You turned around and walked away.

Then I knew I'd lived a lie.

## My Beautiful Son

Walked along a racing line,
Found an entry point
A distance away,
And realised the event horizon.

The flux became a residue,
The mote eye became calm,
Only to be ravaged
By blood-wire technology.

Golgotha. Three days after.
Found the stage,
Fought the praise
And remained ever amazed.

## A Sage Jigsaw

Perhaps I thought I'd only drink there.
Or I was drunk in thought of mind.
Or perhaps I'd lived there, centuries ago.
And ignored it all, stayed blind.
I thought I'd lived in old time Barcelona.
I thought I'd lived in downtown Los Angeles.
I thought I'd lived in old time Catalunya.
But, I guess I did not.
And I guess you've never seen them anyway.

But I can hear sage singing of angels,
Even when the triptych is closed.
And I can hear the wrath of anger
When the jigsaw fails to close.

## Black Hope

Outside
Somewhere,
Somebody is killing the stars.
Surely killing
Like famine.

All the stars
Are being extinguished
One by one.
But a woman is pregnant.
She will have a son.

Just a short walk away
From humanity.

# The Meadow of Atë

This devastating feeling
During my moments of madness, becomes
Numb beauty
On the tightrope edge.

Nebula stars,
Echoes away
Sound aching loneliness
Like Amazonian water falling
Into its timeless well.
Echoing.

Reverence paid
For an empty holding
Whilst kneeling and crying.
Salt water pouring
Shoestring arid attachment.
Fraying hemp commitment
Smouldering tundra fire
White snow wilderness
In the Meadow of Atë.

## Alcoholic

Why resist?
You are only stalling
The inevitable
Life in the gutter.

Incoherent rancid speech.
Intermittent stutters.
Splendid tolerance.
Intimate social dance.
Transcended relief.
Pathological belief.

Theinevitableuncommitteddestruction
Ofareasonableexistence.

# Pas de Deux

i. **Hurricane**

Hurricane storm.
Calm eye rampage.
Thousand yard malice.

I buried you yesterday.
And outside,
Harm is rushing.

ii. **Consequence**

It is starkly apparent
That some fears are rational
And some are not.
Some find theirs, too late.

But mine.
Cauterised my soul.

iii. **One Day, Only One Year**

And on the edge
Above comprehension,
Is that feeling
Of available destruction.

Hurl yourself towards
Imminent, intimate
Apparition.

And rather live
In a world of magic,
Where honour and love
Are real.
Instead of this one.
Of one thousand shimmering whispers.

## Replenish My Atmosphere

I drink blood-tinged ochre history,
I view my friends from afar.

I feel now. I am ready to account for
The replete expectation
Of acid life,
But with certain reservation:

Like cancer.
That can strike. And take you away.
Like mind numb
Crass idiocy
Destroying ability.
Like degeneration
Of lithe mind rapidity.

(But a child's view of heaven
Is sleek lined golden furniture.
Yet, so far no angels have been found,
Though astronauts have lived death,
Beyond the realms of normal breathing).

Expert in appliance,
Corrected in agility,
Stalking oxygen
For selfish validity.

## Snapshot

Out on the street,
Caught a snapshot.
Of a dustman.
Muck and ability.

Caught sight of a child,
Being dragged,
By hand.
A disconsolate possession.

Found a billboard,
Broken and old,
Faded by the sun.
With a picture of Gatsby on it.

There are dust motes in the sunlight,
They rise from the board, drifting from the eyes.
Off the old paper,
They hang in the air.

Like the American Dream.

*ii. Depth*

## Maybe Just An Irish Song

Heard an Irish voice,
Just in passing,
Maybe a song.
Just a reminder of a friend.

Heard an Irish voice.
Just the other day.
Made an impression.
One that stayed.

# More

### *Arrival*
A political consciousness marketed as coherency
Fought by obtrusiveness and unfounded in reality
Means feelings are caught out with bounded rationality;
Didactics of faith and the idiocy of poverty,
Crisis, war, terror and futility.

### *Paradox*
The broken expectation of the majority,
Has seen the extension of criminality,
and the retrospection of chemical anguish.
Conclusion: hope diminishment.

### *Internment*
The clash of wills resumed a war broken only by interlude,
defined by ill-formed rationalisation, bonded by Reformation,
enlightenment, moral rectitude and blood.

The breaking of youth, of nations,
characterised by the slaying of Abel, wooden hut camps, and the
poetry of soldiers has evolved into irrationality, breaking the word of
God, national critical structural peace, brotherhood, faith.

### *Regression*
In 1976
The streams dried up, but there was no famine here.
Innocently playing in dry river bed ecstasy,
The child threw stones at his friends
And played sword-fighting,
Cowboys and Indians.
Not knowing the re-enactment of
Internecine strife was prophetic.

### Weakness
The Wailing Wall, the beating of temple, the crying mothers, the critical exam, the morally corrupt failure consciousness, the fealty of honour crushed by liberalism,
The selfishness of self.
All failure generated doublespeak amnesiac denial.

### Monolithic
Dark stone throne, power choice emancipation.
The bone weapon striking friendly brains.

### Choice?
One man died for no reason, crying for help, without choice.
And he was afraid.

### Strength
The bitter clash is coming to swallow the faithful
Who missed the clarion call for downfall,
And the proclamation for breaking faith,
And welcoming crisis and death.

Whilst you weep for such moral weakness,
Nations allowed themselves to be broken by the few.

And the strong will be lambasted for pre-emption, survival and the revenge of dead children.

## Talk or Listen

Happening as it is,
Is the ability to be,
As you are, when you are,
Where you want to be.

Lets talk individuality,
Actuality
And the reason to be.

Above all, is seeing,
Consequence
In aspiration,
Part use and ability
Possible adversity,
Checking out scenes
And seeing finality.

## The Photographic Room

As farewells were played,
Order became disorder
And sciamachy took root.

In the dark place, where mirrors
Refracted black light
Breathing became ragged.

Now though. Oxygen rips
into dying vessels.
Under protest. In conflict with
Arcing strand flash memory.

And, I, cannot now
Recognise a face.
There is but a record
Of a dark place.

And the dead banjo player
Strums discordant notes -
Breaking harmony, history,
Calling misery, shunning bliss strategy -
Saying goodbye.
To another's philosophy.

## You Women Who Have Lived In Me

You women who have lived in me
Have sometime discovered yourselves
Within the consummate sexual act.
Partly out of self gratification
Partly out of sharing.

You, sitting, holding hands.
Do you love the person you sit with?
You do?
Well then, time to prepare
For the inevitable terror of being alone.
The crushing impact
Of being a child again.

Can't you understand
That ever within harmony
There is a maelstrom of violence?
Reverent crucifixion.

You women have lived in me.
You must believe in rabid
Sanity.

# The One-Eyed Queen

Do you believe
In plain old communication?
I once did, so did you,
Then you started stalling.

Perhaps you felt it,
Although less acutely than I.
For I was the blind man,
You, the one-eyed queen.

It felt like my heart was raped,
I saw ease in ways to die.
I scrabbled for hope on all sides
No, was the reply.

## Apart

Think of all the time wasted
When your heart
Is coming through your throat
Ripping, arterial bleeds spouting
Gobbets of love
As you sweat rivers into your sheets
Unable to wake
Or scale the cliffs
Of your suffocating panic.

Think of all the time wasted
When all that is important
Has floated away,
In the blinking of a crazed eye.
As you dream of a love
You can never have.
Because it died.

## Haunt Me

Just one minute strand
Of indecipherable
Spider incandescence
Capture emission is,
With the wherewithal of
True gaol: rapture.

There was a song.
It meant nothing.
Unless you listened to
The passion
Of it singing purity.

Saw the web. Bound up and
Caught the flame.
Could not
Close the deal.

## Examine

There it is. The ability to cry.
The ability to die.
The ability to try.
The stability to strive.
And the requisite respiration
Just to stay alive.

Caught you suddenly.
Caught you too soon.
For an absolute will
To edge and dive.

## Cannon

Ruptured arrival,
Like a gunshot wound.
Unexpected and sudden.

Like travesty.
Imprinted like scars.

Apparition. Peace pipe.
Be afraid. Be more afraid
Of lovers and friends,
Than of anyone else.

More than anybody.

## Halve My Life, Quarter My Thought

Slake my thirst,
My hunger, the rage.
The glimpse of freedom,
Apart and away
From the covering veil.

A shredding tremor,
Seeking a bed of finite splendour,
And a masthead
Upon which to be crowned,
Where the sun shrieks to smote a god's eye,
Moves,
Smitten with revenge
And mighty strings of dread
and hollow dirt.

Cut me in quarters.
Better to spread the dissolute thought;
Split the capability to frame the atom rebellion,
Or yet, dissolve the glue which
Holds the fragments,
Which hold all gems, all gold, all we revere, all we seek as precious.

Frame a new picture as the cutter cuts the ocean,
And the waves strike the shore and
The infinite paths, the intimate branches, the nucleus accumbens,
The divided blood rust souls.

Redemption is at hand;
Endless nirvana, settlement, calm.
To wash away the fragments and the bone and the dust
And the confusion.

Split me in half,
See what you find;
The unknown giant and
The blind leading the blind.

*iii. War*

## Roman Catholic

It was August,

The faithful application of human consequence.

All that caused it,

Was a momentary practice of brutality.


Death occurred on Golgotha,

It was an illusion forgiveness,

And all favoured escape.

All was crisis authority,

By guilt and by faith.


Further your imagination

By nothing more

Than saying fright is power.

And power is control.

## Judgement Has Found You Worthy

Hold fast,
The King of kings has spoken.
Hold fast when you fight your gods,
Your monsters and windmills,
Just like Don Quixote.

When your sorrowful tear falls upon
The scars of the last wound or death,
And you cannot see for blurred, devastated vision,
Leave no man behind.

When you walk with the bold,
In certain knowledge,
Hold fast for you're the dying proof of sacrifice.

Your bleeding side parallels another,
And crying will not save you.

Hold fast and you will have a beautiful grave.

## Stealing Stars

When the maelstrom strikes,
With you laden of hope,
And it holds you fixed
Pray for courage and salvation.

A cold headstone.
In the middle of France,
Or the heat of the empire,
Or a forgotten field,
Or in the cool green of home,
Because the King of Kings
Has spoken.

And taken you away
And stolen a star.

## On Investigating Dreams

Hypodermic skin puncture.
Blood stabbing hot flushing
Rage ability.

I wondered when the past
Would stop.
Kind of saw it now.
Waited for it then.
Wished for it before.
Found it in the depths of
recent, able history.

Hip, astute, coarse
and blind,
I'd like to be able
To crave death alive.
I think I've found it.
I think I've seen.
Crime, favour, love
And a dream.

## God Allows An Angel To Die

It was Tuesday.
A heart stopped
At the end of your phone call.
It was so sudden.

Behind a rage of windows
A sea of faces
Prayed for your descent.
Just before the collapse
Of what we all knew.

I saw no wings
Snapshot man,
During your angel fall.

# The Great Debate

### *Entrée*
Churchill said,
"We must defeat evil."
And Jesus agreed.

Ghandi said,
"But it must be achieved peacefully."
Hope agreed.

Kofi said,
"Of course, but, this must be debated."
Conan disagreed.

He said,
"In battle, valour is all,
And the lamentations of the women mean victory."

But on the day Wilfred Owen died,
Siegfried cried,
And the table sat in silence.

### *The Main Course*
Vera said,
"We'll meet again."
Tommy disagreed.

"My friends are dead,"
He said.
And God agreed.

He said,
"So is my son, and the fault is mine."
Futility agreed.

Faith retorted,
"Good may come of this."
And Mohammed went to the mountain,

But the mountain maintained
Neutrality.
And never spoke.

### Dessert
Jesus rose and opened the tomb.
Torquemada opened discussion,
And nobody disagreed.

Then dessert was served,
It was truly exquisite, delightfully sweet,
Conversation lulled.

### Après
After dinner, talk resumed.
As smoke curled and swam
Amongst the old wood beams,
And the fumes from an excellent year
Dulled the senses.
A remark was heard,
"Enough talk, it is time for action."

The silent four horsemen,
Reluctant guests,
Grinned.
"We agree," they said.

## A Reckoning

Flying over the Potomac
And away from the heart
Of the American Dream, was
Like crossing the Rubicon.
There was no turning back.

The shadowed hope of an ally,
And dreams of our glory and history,
Beckon, but do not deny
The fragility of adventure.

The creature of memory
Holds a picture which depreciates
All happiness, all fear.

And in the heat; acceptance,
Whilst the lights burn bright at home.

And in the bloody dust; redemption.

## The Promise Of Things To Come

*Hüzün* haunts me,
It rises impatient,
Weaving inside my heart,
Calling to my soul.

Only the foolish desire,
Moments of frantic fear, amongst
Shards, flying almost by instinct,
Hissing, spitting furious
Flechettes and heat
Shedding copper jacketed poison,
Inverting and shredding the air.

Who would choose such a fate?
With nothing to show
But memories of pain,
A glint of hanging metal
Broken fragments of triumph,
And only blood to slake the serpent,
With the promise of things to come.

## Do Not Hesitate

"The god of war hates
Those who hesitate."
But he hates the vanquished more.
Not for him the dishonourable and weak,
But the chosen, the glorious fallen and the victor.

When you see one thousand leopards
Storming from the sun,
You know you are in Valhalla,
And somehow your luck went wrong;
The bullet, the IED, the rocket,
The child suicide bomber.

Not for the soldier is luxury.
Only the choice to pull the trigger,
To take the next step on unsafe terrain,
To look for the enemy,
To choose to save a life,
To choose to take one.

Do not hesitate soldier.
It could be your last mistake.
Your reward would be expiration and enmity
Of the god of war,
For he hates the indecisive.

## Of The Oleander

There is one blade of grass
Growing on your grave,
In the dust from 1941.
The gunner on your right –
A howitzer man,
The pilot on your left -
He once flew into the sun.
Both fell when the attacks came in.

The verandahs now lie in disarray,
Trees unkempt, the troops long gone.
Rutted roads lead to the missing epitaphs,
Which read like a message from the dead,
'Here we lie, not the first, not the last,
Defiled in a broken land.'

In Habbaniyah,
The *Nerium* wept oleandrin and neriine poison
Whilst the *muntahik hurmat el kibor*
Desecrated the graves
Of your Abyssinian comrades.

The dust is still on Armistice Day,
It is heavy on the ground,
Despite the breeze,
Which once fanned
The soldiers and airmen
Of the Oleander.

## The Boneyard

The Boneyard at Taji
Holds the detritus of war.
Lost and dangerous toys, skeletons
Seeking their previous owners,
Whose stories are embedded
In the rusting metal,
Just as metal was embedded
In them.

If only the silent hulks
Could speak of the
Interior terror, the sweat,
Of glad hails of fleeting victory,
And the darkness and
Sporadic tracer light,
Before their own demise.

Burnt and scoured by the sun,
The messages of aftermath
Are written on their sides,
With a graffiti of love,
Hope and comedy.
But the broken toys
Would weep if they could,
The same as their ancestors
At Normandy and El Alamein.
And they would speak of fragility
And honour,
And furious pain.

# The Baghdad Cigar Aficionado Club

The Baghdad Cigar Aficionado Club
Always starts with a prayer
For families, for hope
And then for the brethren.
Later, there is silent recognition of
The sudden explosion beyond our walls
And the firefight flashes on the horizon.

Overhead, the medevac helos
Always sound angry, especially at night,
Engines roaring a protest
Against the misery of their cargo,
As they fly to their grim sanctuary of hope,
With crewmen full of purpose and pity.

At the Baghdad Cigar Aficionado Club,
Many wish the leaf they burn
Was the causal afterglow
Of those distant firefights,
As the aromatic smoke drifts
Upward, toward the rotor wash,
Laden with unspoken gratitude that
They, are in a safe camaraderie, and
The medevac crews are not, for now,
Mopping up their blood.

## Option Was Zero

My past heart was reft by an outside decision.
It was not seen.
Nor was it an envisaged event.
But it was simple and devastating.

Respondent synapses reacted
And struck like a bomb, which
Exploded rationale, and
Detonated shrieking pain.

No sense,
No answer,
No escape,
No closure.

Crime ran high in theory,
Contempt was tried, and
Options examined, but
Turned to zero.

Future remains
Blurred.

## The Battle List & The Way Ahead

I would like to have seen
The fights at the Marne, Delvilles Wood, Beaumont Hamell,
And the last great cavalry battle of Meggido,
In all their heroic, tragic glory
As long as I survived.

And all of the others; the inexhaustible list.
The Somme, Sangin, Singapore,
Isandlwana, Basrah, Lucknow, Vimy Ridge
The Crimea, Musa Qala, Waterloo,
Goose Green, Rorkes Drift, Kajaki Dam,
Normandy, Ortona, Al Amarah, Zungeni Mountain,
The Rhine Crossing, Ypres, Hong Kong, Habbaniyah.

A few of many. Say enough of them
And the metronomic effect
Dulls the pain. Strengthens resolve.
Harkens to glory; in defeat or victory.

The battle list is long my friend, but
It is longer for the dead,
And it is not over yet.
For by example, we lead.

## The Conservation of Angular Momentum

If you lined the Appian Way
With the souls on crosses
Of all of our dead soldiers,
And had the widows grieving
At their spectral feet,
What a monument to God it would be;
A multitude replica of Golgotha.

Is it hubris to think
There is poetry in the slaying of enemies,
But there is no respite from lust?
For everywhere there are reminders
Of fragility and mortality,
Of paradise lost and of a desert *Mastema*
And a tornado of fallen men,
Reaching, arms outstretched
Into an empty sky.

*iv. Regicide*

## Enemy

As the tide came in,
The comprehension of transient breath became
Unmistakable.

As the sail unfurled,
The flying flag responded to
An immature wind.

Once buffeted, the dispersed air floated away,
Only to be breathed by an unwitting person,

Who could be the butterfly of our people.
Or like any individual,
The enemy of our soul.

## Murder

There is murder in my heart.
There is murder in my heart.
There is fury in my heart.

There is murderous fury in my heart.
There is murderous fury in my heart.
There is pain in my heart.

There is furious pain in my heart.
There is furious pain in my heart.
And there is one just solution.

## Silver Traitor

The breath left the body,
It could no longer breathe.
The weight was overflowing.

Salt became liquid,
Shortly after hollowness.
The emptiness was holistic.

The deal broke collaboration,
The demise of alliance,
Is suffocating.

## Oracle

My heart has found a path uneasy on the road,
Uneasy on the norm or the conviction of convention
But to it, I must lie.

If I could speak the language of dark angels,
Or hum eulogy to tragic regret,
Maybe my heart will find rest
Before I die,
But I suspect not,

I suspect I cannot find
An easy tread or easy faith,
Or anything simple
On which to succour a weary heart.

From where in my heart of angel love gold
Do I find my peace; or the calling
When my penance is done and I enter heaven?
And when my tribe is open and grown,
Praying over my grave,
Will they ever forgive me and for what?

The hymn of destruction is apposite;
The call of beauty; the speech, the blood,
Fealty and betrayals,
Our life and the way,

Hold me close
When I cry and my heart breaks.
Envelop me in subliminal bliss
And dark matter algebra.
Kiss me with a passion
That makes my heart explode.

Hold me my love,
My beautiful one,
Hold me until I expire,
Until I fold.

## That Killing Feeling

Insurgent, emotional
Blood-spiralling
DNA.

Sometimes
I pray euphoric
Emptiness fades.

Bleeding.
Flying ash,
Flowing freely.

Today is not a good day for me.
I wish I'd never lived it.
It was enough to
Kill anybody.

## Remorse (Hoc Majorum Virtus)

'What hath God wrought'
But the means of majesty?
Imperial in its fearsome energy
Is the glory of my ancestors.
With each dying limb,
Crumbling, dust-like
Silhouette ashes, all.

What hath man wrought
But denial and futility?
What hath he wrought
Through the crescent of stars,
Far off, insane with hope
But hampered by fragility,
Sloth and avarice,
Nor recognition of the bow wave
And strings to manipulate survival,
From our ultimate remorse.

## As the Empire Falls

There will be a thousand questions,
At the end of my fallen empire.

There will be no satisfactory answer.
There will be no empirical surprise.
No surfeit of thought,
No space.

A short wonder about God,
And then,
A cataclysm,
As the supremacy disrupts.

# v. The Keening

## The Availability of the Dead

And there was an equal amount of pain.
As everybody was available.

But the line was short.
It was all based on supposition,
In order to formulate a gathering
Of the definitive, soon available dead.

They walked through ploughed field,
They traipsed through bone.
They were smashed and shattered.
And formed a collective show.

How to fight desperate tears?
When presence means nothing to the ghosts.
How to say hello to the dead?
Who are available in droves.

## Quick Blood Fasting

My blood was thin.
It pumped quickly.
And flooded my heart.

The blood was quick.
My soul gave way.
I held it all apart.

I saw you brave.
I saw you fly.
I saw you go.
And said goodbye.

My blood ran cold.
My heart stopped.
I could have held you close.

## Stone-God Heart

My mute sorrow
Could break the heart
Of a stone-god,
And a thousand tears
Cannot bring you back.

At rest under black onyx,
There is no reflection
Of a seething anger,
The lack of necessity,
Or explanation.

No prayer can sanction
Such history, such tragedy.
No answer can slake
The thirst for vengeance
In paradise.

All is lost now my lovely,
All is gone.
The stone-god has shattered
His heart, and the splinters
Have shredded immortality,
As naught but a lie.

## The Cross Of Hope Is Broken

I drove five hundred and sixty six miles,
Along a trail strewn with husks
And seeds of doubt,
And the deafening silence of a dead child

My destination was a house
Of false hope and silence.

Underneath a raging explosion of purple cherry blossom
The sun still shines upon you.
But the cross of hope is broken,
Mired with sorrow,
And I will sit by your grave,
Mourn you for eternity
And weep.

## To Lament The Dead

And I will
Read your soul,
And love you,
In devastating fashion.

And I will sail
A tall ship
Across monster oceans,
And dead calm oblivion
Rage scene surf
And stop.

And I wail hard
And see whales
And hold stars
And be alive to
The fact that I,
Can hurt a living
Individual
Without even trying.

## Where Your Ashes Kiss The Earth

At the end, a flag and your medals,
And a salute, brother.
Perhaps, there will be
An Enochian song,
A welcoming on high.
For you. One of our own.

In glacial millennia,
We are as naught but dust
After our halcyon days;
Carefree, lustful and invincible,
With the energy of the sun.
But in a thousand years,
Where your ashes kiss the earth,
Perhaps you will be remembered
As a man amongst men.
But no more so than now,
As we weep with your widow.

Perhaps our mute sorrow will
Be salute enough for you, friend,
And the wild savagery that follows
Your sombre burning, will be
Our keening of gratitude,
For one of our own.

## Breathless Delight

When I am old,
I'd like to die
With no diffident crawl.

When I am old,
I'd prefer to go
Without the ache.

When I am old,
And my mind has gone,
I'll have heard the
Siren calling.

When I am old,
And my friends are gone,
Let me go to them.

And when I have lived,
And when I have cried,
Just let me sigh.
My last life of breath,
My aching goodbye;
My last testimony of friendless delight.

(I won't feel remorse.
I won't feel guilt.
I won't regret
My effortless passing,
Or envy of the chine.)

# Epilogue

## A Million To One

Did you find
Ghost,
That my heart left you
When you said goodbye?

Did you break your own heart
Ghost,
Because we cannot?

Can you love a million people
Ghost.
Or do you choose just one?
Why would you want to,
Ghost?

## Appendix: Notes

*Ryan Gearing, my publisher, asked me to provide some background to my work, which I am happy to do. I make no secret that some of my work is obscure and could be interpreted in a number of ways; I see no issue with this. To that end, where I think too much information would detract from the poem I have been deliberately vague or only provided the date, and in most cases the location of where the poem was written. In other poems, the meaning and references are explicit and this too is deliberate.*

## Prologue

The Blood of Kings. Winter, 1994. It is a lament about the fragility of love and false hope.

## i. Beginning the Reign

Lost in Bohemia. Prague, April 1994.

Opposites Attract. Spring, 1994.

A Small Untruth. 1997. A vision of the moment a heart is broken asunder.

My Beautiful Son. Summer, 2005. A reference to individual potential.

A Sage Jigsaw. Summer, 1989. This has been revised more times than I can remember. Its meaning is closed, like the triptych.

Black Hope. 1998. With acknowledgement to author, David Zindell. A message of hope.

Meadow of Ate. March 1994. In Greek mythology, the goddess Atë, or Ate, is the personification for "ruin, folly, delusion." In her book, *The March of Folly*, Barbara Tuchman notes that the earth has been called The Meadow of Atë.

Alcoholic. 1995. When you stand on the edge...

Pas de Deux. 1993. When someone leaves you...

Replenish My Atmosphere. 1992. A reflection on what it is to be alive.

Snapshot. Skopje, Macedonia, 2006. Literally a snapshot of what I saw on a street in Skopje which led me to thinking about ambition and reality.

## ii. Depth

More. 2005. Originally a stream of consciousness epic, this started as a result of watching numerous documentaries about politics, history and current wars. I condensed it to show the interrelation of all things and the futility of weakness.

Maybe Just An Irish Song. 1988/2003, Belfast. Written about a friend, if she is reading this, she'll know who she is.

Talk Or Listen. 1994. Germany. The endless debate about who we are.

The Photographic Room. 1994, Germany. When someone leads your heart and then leaves it...

You Women Who Have Lived In Me. 1991, Paddington Station, England. Sat in a cafe, watching a crazy, muttering women who was obviously distraught, as if a plague of anguish was rising from her soul.

The One-Eyed Queen. 1997, Cardiff. Reflection on a dead relationship.

Apart. 1987, England. This has changed a lot over the years becoming more graphic in its allegorical take on grief over lost love.

Haunt Me. 1994, Germany.

Examine. 1998, Cardiff, Wales.

Cannon. 2003, Canada. Betrayal and lost faith.

Halve My Life, Quarter My Thought. 2011, USA. Reflection on truth and perceptions of reality.

## iii. War

Roman Catholic. 1996, Cardiff. Reflection on religion.

Judgement Has Found You Worthy. 2005, France. Visiting a Commonwealth War Cemetery I saw this inscription on a headstone, "The King of kings has spoken," and this poem was written the same day.

Stealing Stars. 2008, USA. Thinking about my upcoming deployment to Iraq. I deliberately used the 'King of kings' again.

On Investigating Dreams. 1999, Cardiff, Wales. What are dreams really for?

God Allows An Angel To Die. The events of 9/11 took place on a Tuesday. The 'snapshot man' died whilst leaping from one of twin towers and was photographed in flight. His identity, as far as I am aware has never been discovered. The documentary '9/11 The Falling Man' was the catalyst for this poem.

The Great Debate. 2006. Once the Iraq war started in 2003, I started the outline and concept of this poem; it took 3 years to find the right cast of players. The 'quote' by Conan is taken from the movie, "Conan The Barbarian."

A Reckoning. 2008, en route from USA to UK. Written as I was flying the first leg of my inbound deployment to Iraq.

The Promise of Things to Come. Baghdad, 7 Oct 2008. *Hüzün* is a Turkish word with an Arabic root, meaning, in its simplest sense, melancholy, but in the context of the poem, it is more a philosophy of military spirituality and life.

Do Not Hesitate. Germany 2009. The quote, *"The God of War hates those who hesitate,"* is attributed to Euripides, 480-406 BC. Written after hearing the news about a child suicide bomber in Afghanistan.

Of The Oleander. Habbaniyah, Iraq, 11 November 2008. Nerium is the latin genus for oleander. *Oleandrin* and *neriine* poison are products of the Oleander plant, all parts of which are extremely poisonous. '... *muntahik hurmat el kibor*' is Arabic and means literally 'grave invader and trespasser.' Sometime between 2003-2004 some Iraqi muslims desecrated the graves of the Abyssinian Christian Iraqis who fought and died alongside their British and Commonwealth allies in WWII in the Battle of Habbaniyah in 1941. The cemetery at Habbaniyah is one of many Commonwealth Cemeteries in Iraq. Some 52,400 Commonwealth military personnel died in Iraq in the Second World War.

The Boneyard. Taji and Baghdad, 21-23 Oct 2008. The evocative scrapyards at Taji were filled with broken, bombed and destroyed tanks, howitzers, trucks and other military hardware. It was an evocative place and in its own way a memorial to the men who had died and been wounded whilst fighting in those vehicles and using that equipment.

The Baghdad Cigar Aficionado Club. 11 Oct 2008, Baghdad. With acknowledgement to Prince Sined Yar Maharg of fabled Xanadu.

Option Was Zero. 2009, Andover, England. The reaction to things that happen outside of your control which could be applied equally to being at war or affairs of the heart.

The Battle List & The Way Ahead. July 2009, Germany. A reflection on British Army history and a view of the future.

The Conservation of Angular Momentum. 2010, Nicosia, Cyprus. The vortex of death as a soldier with an acknowledgement to Milton and the savagery of the Roman Empire. *Mastema:* According to the book of Jubilees, Mastema "Hostility" is the chief of the demons engendered by the fallen Watchers/Angels with women, perhaps one of those same demons. His actions and name indicate he is the Satan, the 'Adversary', but much more the Satan who appears in the book of Job with a function to fulfil under God than the Satan of later tradition who is the uttermost enemy of God. (Definition from Wikipedia).

## iv. Regicide

Enemy. 2000, Episkopi, Cyprus. Reflection on the philosophical nature of a potential adversary.

Murder. 2001, Germany. The thought process which results when hearing something which literally drives you to murderous rage in an instant.

Silver Traitor. 1994, Germany. The silver traitor is Judas; he or she comes in many forms.

That Killing Feeling. 1995, England. Reflection on depression.

Oracle. 2010, Nicosia, Cyprus. Love, death and religion.

Remorse (Hoc Majorum Virtus). 2002, Glasgow, Scotland. The quote, *"What hath God wrought"* is said to be the first public telegram in America, sent by Samuel Morse in 1844.

As The Empire Falls. 2006, Stanmore, England.

## v. The Keening

The Availability of the Dead. 2000, The Somme, France.

Quick Blood Fasting. 2005, England. The rush of adrenaline when you think you have lost somebody.

Stone-God Heart. 2010, Germany. The false hope of immortality and resultant, seething grief.

The Cross Of Hope Is Broken. 2010, Germany. In memory of my niece, Jeni Rose. Jeni died in January 2010, aged 17.

To Lament The Dead. 1998, England.

Where Your Ashes Kiss the Earth. 24 December 2008, Iraq. Dedicated to my friend, Lieutenant Colonel Neil Lewis RLC, Commanding Officer 27 Regt RLC. Neil died on 23 Dec 2008.

Breathless Delight. 2001, Germany. When fate decrees it, just let go.

# Epilogue

A Million To One. 2010, Germany. The ghost knows.

ND - #0331 - 270225 - C0 - 210/148/6 - PB - 9781908487216 - Matt Lamination